KiDS n' KATALOGS

By Louise Weber
M. C. Weber

ISBN 913916-24-2
Library of Congress Catalog Card Number 76-20953

Printed in Nashville, Tennessee
by Incentive Publications
Box 12522
Nashville, Tennessee 37212

TABLE OF CONTENTS

I   WORD RECOGNITION EXPERIENCES

Sight Vocabulary

Association and Discrimination

II WORD MEANING EXPERIENCES

Usage

Context Clues

III WORD ANALYSIS EXPERIENCES

Structural Analysis

Phonics

IV   COMPREHENSION EXPERIENCES

Critical Thinking

Using References

V CREATIVE EXPERIENCES

Oral Expression

Written Expression

Note For The Teacher

Kids n' Katalogs presents activities and ideas for developing and reinforcing reading skills in the elementary school. All of the activities are based on the use of mail-order catalogs and do not require additional commercial materials. The learning experiences are designed to develop the major skills of word recognition, word meaning, word analysis, comprehension, and communication. Since these are the same skill areas identified in many current reading programs, Kids n' Katalogs can be used to supplement most reading approaches.

For convenience and consistency in teaching, all activities are written with the same format. Each will provide: the title, the skill purpose, preparation directions, procedure for implementation, and extension activities. Each activity is designated either for primary or intermediate learning levels. However, these suggested levels are only approximations. As teachers of reading, we know that every group, large or small, reflects variations in individual skill development and reading achievement. Any activity, then, may be adjusted to meet differing student needs.

The teaching-learning strategies used in the book vary. Some call for the simultaneous participation of the total class, while others are intended for independent use by small groups or individual students. Several activities are designed to be played as games. Teacher work time for preparing the activities has been minimized. Suggestions are offered whereby the students can assume much of the preparatory work as learning experiences.

Note that methods and criteria for evaluating student success have been omitted. We have purposely done this because of student individuality. Evaluative methods can't really be generalized to the extent that they will apply to all teaching-learning situations. Teachers know their own students better than any other teacher and can, therefore, more effectively evaluate their work.

With this brief introduction we wish you success with Kids n' Katalogs. We hope you and your students will enjoy the activities.

Louise Weber
M. C. Weber

Preparation:

A. The students must know how to use the catalog's index before doing this activity.

B. Select several broad categories into which catalog items can be placed. Three suggested categories are sports, pets, and shoes.

C. On the chalk board or on large sheets of paper, draw large outline pictures depicting each category heading. On each of these, write the heading and the names of several items in that category. List items which would be unknown to the students. Drawings might look similar to those below:

Procedure:

A. Read the names of the category headings to the students.

B. Direct each student to choose one category, find pictures of the items listed in that category, cut them from the catalog, and paste them on the appropriate outline picture.

9

Extension:

Students might prepare their own categories, including the individual items in each.

WHAT'S MY NAME?

Preparation:

A. Select from the catalog pictures of twenty different items which would be unfamiliar to students.

B. Paste each picture to a large index card. Write four different item names, one of which is the actual name, below the picture. Number each card for identification and place all cards in an envelope. Include an answer key card for self-checking.

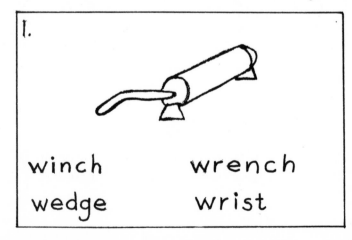

1.

winch   wrench

wedge   wrist

1. winch
2. barometer
3. router

19. sconce
20. awl

Procedure:

Direct students to use the catalog index to locate each item named. By comparing each catalog picture with that on the card, he can determine the correct name of the item on the card.

Extension:

A. Each student might select from the catalog a less familiar item to use as part of a class guessing game.

B. The activity might be reversed by directing the students to find pictures of an unfamiliar item name. (The catalog index would be used in finding pictures of the item.)

Suggested words:

lathe	binoculars	goggles
bassinet	auger	gasket
ladle	culotte	parquet
dado set	chandelier	hydrometer
bellows		coverlet

WORD PICKERS

Preparation:

Write twenty adjectives on the chalk board. Include words of varying difficulty for the students. The word list might be similar to the following:

big	round	shiny	straight
red	colorful	slick	tall
smelly	bleak	smooth	rough
pretty	faded	loud	rugged
flat	green	fluffy	fantastic

Procedure:

A. Read the list of words to the students, explaining that the words may be used to describe catalog items.

B. Then direct each student to cut out pictures of any five items and glue them to individual sheets of paper.

C. The students may select appropriate words from the prepared list to describe each picture or use descriptive words of their own. The words are to be written below each picture.

D. Each student might show one picture to the class and read the selected words which describe the pictured item.

Extension:

Students might write riddles about several of the items. These may be read to the other class members.

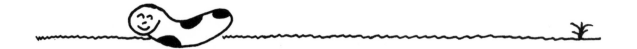

DOODLERS

Preparation:

A.   Write the word "Doodles" on the chalk board with colored chalk or on a large sheet of mural paper with tempera paint.

B.   Section the board or paper into the same number of spaces as there are students in class. Direct each student to label his own space.

Procedure:

A.   Select a catalog page number at random and direct the students to locate that page in their catalogs.

B.   Direct the students to read several item descriptions from that page to locate descriptive words that lend themselves to "doodling".

C.   The student then draws "doodles" of these words in his own space.

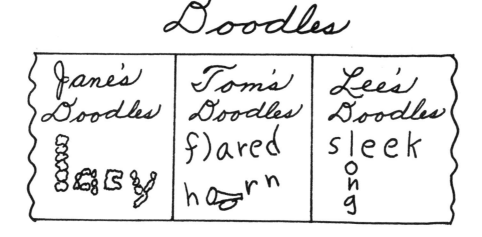

Extension:

A. Encourage the students to try reading each other's "doodles".

B. Place limits on the kind of words which can be written in the "doodle" spaces, i.e., (1) the number of syllables in the words, (2) the words must relate to a particular category as sports or pets, or (3) the words can begin only with particular letters, etc.

MATCH THIS !

Sight Vocabulary
Primary Level

Preparation:

A. Cut out twenty small catalog pictures and mount them on small pieces of cardboard. Rule a piece of poster board into two vertical columns and twenty horizontal sections. In the left column write the names of the items you have mounted; leave the right column blank.

B. Attach an answer key to the back of the poster.

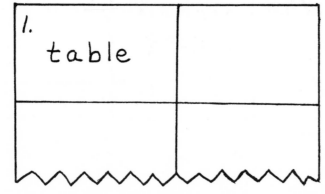

Procedure:

Direct students to match mounted pictures with their correct names by placing them opposite the appropriate name on the chart.

Extension:

A. The activity might be reversed by mounting pictures on the poster board and asking students to write in the names.

B. The students might construct their own item—name groups for matching and then exchange these with other class members.

COLLECTORS' ITEMS

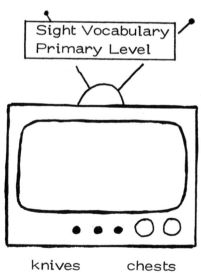

Preparation:

A. Before the activity, draw a mock television screen on a large piece of poster board. Cut out the screen area.

B. Write twenty familiar item names on individual flash cards. Suggested words are:

coat	hat	bowl	curtains	table	knives	chests
boat	jeans	shirt	clock	tire	lamp	caps
shoes	socks	pillow	shorts	wagon	jacket	

Procedure:

A. Divide the class into teams.

B. Hold each flash card in the television screen for only two minutes. During this period each student may collect as many pictures of the item as possible from his catalog. The team which collects the most pictures by the end of the activity will be declared the winners.

Extension:

The procedures might be reversed by showing a picture of an item through the screen and then directing the teams to write as many names or uses as possible for that particular item.

PUZZLE BREAKERS

Sight Vocabulary
Primary Level

Preparation:

Provide for each student a duplicated copy of an acrostic similar to the one below.

S	ski	
U		
E		

Procedure:

    A. Ask each student to write his name vertically in column one of the acrostic.

    B. The student should search the catalog for items whose names have the same initial letters as those on the acrostic. The names are to be written in the spaces of the middle column.

    C. Pictures of these items may then be pasted in the third column.

Extension:

    A. The activity might be played as a game in which the students work against time in completing the puzzle.

    B. Each student might try reading the completed acrostics of other students.

WORD PIRATES

Sight Vocabulary
Primary Level

Preparation:

    Make a hat pattern which may be used to create a simple "pirate hat" (see **example**).

Procedure:

    A. Direct the students to pretend they are pirates looking for word treasures in the catalogs. Word treasures are words which the student can read.

B. Each student may construct his or her own treasure hat on which the word treasures may be written or pasted.

Extension:

A. Students may exchange hats and try reading each other's word treasures.

B. The treasure hats might be worn the entire school day with new words being added as they are learned in other learning situations.

C. Limitations may be imposed on just what words may be written on the hats, i.e., number of syllables, descriptive words, action words, etc.

LAUNDRY FUN

Sight Vocabulary
Primary Level

Preparation:

A. Direct each student to cut one picture of a single clothing item from the catalog and paste the picture to heavier paper.

B. Write the names of the clothing items on the chalk board. (The students should not observe this process.)

C. Construct a clothes line by fastening a piece of twine across one corner of the room. This will be used during the activity by the students for hanging pictures of correctly named items. Paper clips may be used to hang the pictures from the line.

Procedure:

A. Show one picture of a clothing item to the class. Invite an individual student to select the correct name of the item from the word list on the chalk board.

B. When an item is correctly named, the student may write the item's name on the picture and hang the picture on the line. The student may also wish to write his or her name on the picture, i.e., washed by Jamie.

SHAPELY SHAPES

Preparation:

A. Write a list of shape words on the chalk board or on large poster board: circle, square, rectangle, triangle, cube, cone, sphere, trapezoid, pentagon, hexagon, etc.

B. The more simple shape words might be used with the younger students while the more able students might be assigned the harder-to-find shapes.

Procedure:

    A.   Direct the students to search their catalogs for pictures of items which represent the shapes identified by the words on the chalk board or poster board.

    B.   Pictures of like shapes may then be pasted on the same page.

    C.   Write the name of the shape across the top of the page and assemble all pages in a simple booklet for students to review and enjoy.

Extension:

    A.   Individual booklets may be restricted to include only items which have the same shape.

  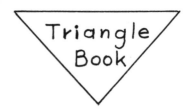

    B.   The students might write sentences using the shape words and include these in the booklets.

    C.   The students might go for a "shape walk" outside the classroom and record the objects which possess a particular shape.

Preparation:

With colored chalk, write on the chalk board in large letters these words: red, blue, yellow, and green. Leave writing space below each word.

Procedure:

A. Introduce the idea that special words are sometimes used in catalog descriptions to describe a particular color or a shade of that color.

B. Divide the students into four teams with each team taking the name of one color word from the chalk board.

C. Direct the students to look for special words used in the catalogs to describe their particular team color. The students may have to look at the picture of the described item in order to determine the indicated color.

D. When a special color word is found, the team member may write it on the chalk board under the appropriate heading.

RED

fiesta
cranberry

BLUE

federal slate
navy

GREEN

celery
avocado

YELLOW

aztec
adobe

Extension:

A. The class might visit a paint store to observe the various names used to describe the different colors of paint.

B. The students might be encouraged to create new names for describing the basic colors of red, green, blue, and yellow.

SUPER SALESMEN

Preparation:

A. Provide materials for students to use in constructing a booklet illustrating the samples of color designs and textures which he or she sells.

B. Prior to the activity discuss the meanings of cloth, material, and clothing. Clothing materials may be described as being plaid, striped, plain, flowery, polka dotted, checked, etc.

Procedure:

A. Direct each "sales person" to prepare a sales booklet which illustrates the different designs and textures of clothing. Pictures of each clothing type may be cut from the catalog and glued to pages in the booklet under the appropriate classification.

B. The booklets might include the following classifications:

Extension:

A. The students might draw a self portrait dressing themselves in the particular type of clothing being worn at the time.

B. Each student may list the color designs and textures found in the parents' closet at home (with the parents' permission).

C. The class might be divided into teams of observers with the members of each team listing the people wearing a particular design or texture that day at school.

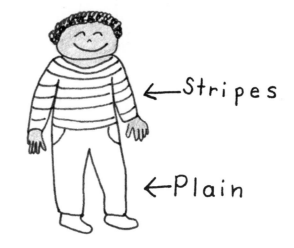

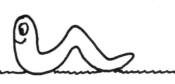

Preparation:

A.   Create a shopping center or mall by painting different kinds of store fronts on large poster board or mural paper. (If a long chalk board is available, this activity may be done with colored chalk.)

B.   Students may assist by working individually or in groups to decorate the store fronts, adding special store names and decorative touches to the different kinds of stores.

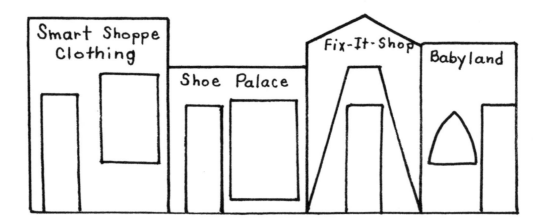

Procedure:

A.   Assign one or more students to be the "manager(s)" responsible for each store. It is their task to decide what kind of merchandise would likely be found in this kind of store and locate similar pictures in catalogs.

B.   Direct the students to cut and paste the pictures of the chosen items on their "stores".

Extension:

A.   This activity might be used as a game, the winners being those who found the greatest number of appropriate items for their stores.

B. Limits might be imposed on the kinds of items to be included in the store inventory: (1) only those items whose names are two-syllable words, (2) only those items whose names begin with vowels, (3) only those items whose names begin with consonant blends, (4) no two items in the store window may begin with the same letter, (5) there must be at least one item in the store window for each letter in the store's name, etc.

C. Students might be encouraged to use the final product (completed stores) in an individualized sight vocabulary-building activity in which each student learned at least ten new words.

D. Students might go "window shopping". Each student might be asked to make a shopping list of items he or she would like to buy. (This may be done with or without the items being labeled.)

PARADE OF HOMES

Association and Discrimination
Intermediate Level

Preparation:

A. Create a "city street" by arranging the students' furniture so that an aisle or "street" separates two rows of furniture.

B. On large poster board or sheets of paper, direct the students to paint replicas of their houses.

C. These home drawings may be taped to the furniture along the street. Invite student ideas for naming the new street.

Procedure:

    A.   Direct each student to cut pictures from the catalog of items found in his or her home and paste the pictures in appropriate places on his home drawing.

    B.   When "homes" have been "furnished", ask each student to label as many of the furnishings as possible.

Extension:

    A.   More able students might draw fairly exact floor plans of their homes and classify item pictures with respect to where the items are located.

    B.   Students might classify their home items according to some special characteristic. The following are suggestions: those items which use energy and those which do not; those which emit noises and those which do not; those which are expensive and those which are not; etc.

INDOORS – OUTDOORS

Association and Discrimination
Primary Level

Preparation:

    Cut several dozen pictures of miscellaneous items from the catalog. (Several students may do this for you.) Mount pictures and place them in a large envelope.

Procedure:

Explain to the students that pictures are to be classified as items used indoors, items used outdoors, or items that may be used either place. An answer key will permit each student to check the accuracy of the completed classification.

Indoors	Outdoors	Either
shower	lawn mower	folding chair
blender	tires	sweater
pillow	hoe	broom
soap	garden hose	screwdriver

Extension:

The activity might be used with other categories, i.e., items used for parties or for everyday, items used during the summer or during the winter, items used at school or at home, etc.

WORD ASSOCIATES

Association and Discrimination
Intermediate Level

Preparation:

A. Direct each student to cut out a picture of a single item and paste it near the top of a page.

B. The student may then take the page to the teacher who prints several words below the item. Some of these words will be associated with the item and some will not. (Five or six words for each item should be adequate, depending upon the student's capability.)

Procedure:

A. Direct each student to read the words written below the item and circle only those which are associated with the item.

B. Completed papers may be evaluated by the teacher.

leather
paper
tassle
strap

buckle

Extension:

A. Students might select and write additional words associated with the pictured item.

B. A contest might be conducted in which the student who adds the most associated words would be recognized as "outstanding word associator".

C. Pictures might be exchanged so other students might read the associated words.

PICK-A-PAIR

Preparation:

    Review possible combinations of items which are used together. A partial list could include the following: knife and fork; pencil and paper; shoes and socks; flowers and pots; saucer and cup; ball and bat. (Your students will probably find some you hadn't thought of.)

Procedure:

A.   Begin the activity by discussing the meaning of "go-together-items". Explain that certain items are often used together.

B.   Direct students to search their catalogs for pictures of items which are used together, cut them out, and paste them together on a sheet of paper.

C.   Each student may share his or her collection of paired items with the class.

Extension:

A.   Time limits might be imposed for finding picture pairs. Students with most items might be recognized.

B.   Paired items might be used as story starters. Example: One day the knife couldn't find the fork. (Students may finish writing the stories.)

Preparation:

    A.   Required pictures may be prepared by directing each student to cut out one picture and paste it onto a card.

    B.   These are handed to the teacher who will cut each picture in half. Each part may be marked with matching numbers on the back side, and picture halves may be placed in a large envelope.

Procedure:

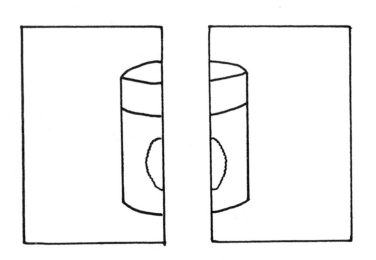

Present the envelope to the students, and explain that whole pictures may be reconstructed by matching the correct picture halves.

Extension:

    A.   Students might reconstruct "funny items" by putting together halves that do not belong together. A new name for those objects might be invented. (Bike wheels paired with a toy car might be named a bicycar.)

    B.   More able students might be challenged by cutting pictures into thirds or fourths which would be reconstructed into whole pictures.

    C.   Written words might be substituted for pictures; word halves would then be matched.

QUICK PICKS

Preparation:

A. In this game activity the students will be directed to a particular catalog page from which they will record words that have been selected by the teacher.

B. A word list with corresponding page numbers might be prepared before the activity begins. The following is a suggested list of instructions.

1.	Page 10	– the word dress.
2.	Page 80	– words which begin with ch.
3.	Page 400	– the word and.
4.	Page 16	– words which begin with sh.
5.	Page 24	– the word size.
6.	Page 261	– words which end in t.
7.	Page 39	– the word if.
8.	Page 409	– words which begin with d.

C. A paper badge might be constructed for awarding the winner of the game.

Procedure:

A. Explain the following game rules:

1. The students will be directed to a catalog page where they will look for certain kinds of words.
2. Time limitations will be imposed (the time allowed for each page should be determined by the ability level of the students).
3. Within the allowed time each student may record as many of the special word(s) as can be found.
4. The game's winner will be the student(s) who records the most special words.

B. The "Best Quick Picker" award badge is presented to the winner.

Preparation:

Students may construct sensory booklets containing pictures of items which stimulate the senses. All five senses could be included in a single booklet, or a different booklet could be constructed for each sense.

Procedure:

A. Direct students to collect pictures of items which stimulate any of the five senses. Pictures may then be sorted and pasted to pages which have been labeled with one of the five senses.

B. Illustrated pages may be assembled into booklets and displayed around the room.

Extension:

A. Items which stimulate more than one sense at the same time might be selected for a booklet.

B. This activity could be played as a game in which students would do the picture collecting within a given time period. The winner would be the individual who found the most pictures.

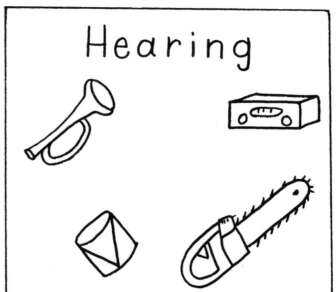

Preparation:

A. A prior class discussion of the term "composition" would be beneficial. Students should be aware that in the context of this activity composition refers to what an item is made of.

B. Outlines of factory buildings may be drawn and colored on the chalk board or on sheets of mural paper. Label each factory with different names: glass factory, wood factory, metal factory, plastic factory, or cloth factory. Leave writing space below each factory's name.

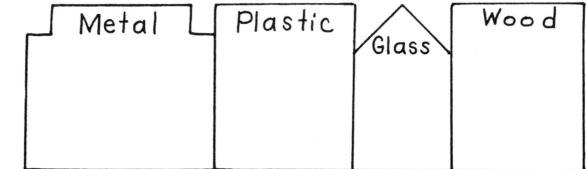

Procedure:

A. Assign students to various factories. Select one as the "manager" of each factory. Students may pretend to be factory workers who are manufacturing products for their particular factory, i.e., wood products, glass products, metal products, etc.

B. Each factory worker is to find and cut out items whose composition corresponds to the type of factory in which each is working. The factory manager will tape or paste these to the factory drawing. Workers may write the item's name next to the pictures they find.

Extension:

The activity might be played as a game in which the winning team would be the one collecting the most items within a pre-selected time period.

Preparation:

A. Mount twelve pictures of single items on individual cards. Cut away the upper right-hand corner in a shape which simulates a puzzle piece. The name of the pictured item is written on this cut-away piece.

B. Place pictures and puzzle pieces in an envelope labeled "Match And Name".

Procedure:

Each student may determine the written name of the pictured item by matching the correct puzzle piece to the original piece of cardboard on which the picture is mounted.

Extension:

Students might prepare their own picture puzzles and exchange them with other students for solving.

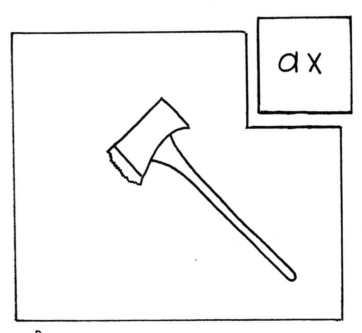

DOUBLE TROUBLE

Preparation:

A. From two identical catalogs cut twelve pairs of identical pictures, i.e., two identical coats, two identical chairs, two identical bicycles, etc. Cut three additional pictures similar but not identical to each identical pair. Example: There would be five pictures of coats, but only two would be identical.

B. Students may paste the pictures on cards. Identical pictures in each category may be labeled on the back with matching letters, i.e., A and A, B and B, etc.

C. Place the sixty pictures (five pictures in twelve categories) in a large envelope and label it "Double Trouble". (For less able students the number of pictures may be reduced.)

Procedure:

A. The collection of mounted pictures may be presented to the class. Explain that some pictures have identical twins in the collection. The task of each student will be to match all identical pictures (twelve pairs).

B. Each student may check completed matches by looking at the corresponding letters on the back of the cards. Correct picture matches will have correct letter matches.

Preparation:

Across the chalk board draw several large outlines of shoe soles. Label each outline with the name of a different shoe type which could be found in the catalog.

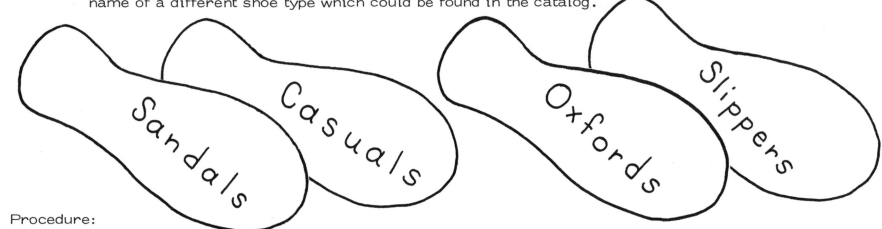

Procedure:

Direct the students to find pictures of the shoe types indicated on the chalk board. These pictures may then be taped to the appropriate shoe type.

Extension:

A. The students might survey their home closets listing the shoe types found.

B. Different classifications might be made on the basis of: shoes for the occasion; shoes for the four seasons; cost of shoe types, etc.

C. Each student might be invited to select a shoe type and tell why he or she likes the shoes.

PUT IT THERE

Preparation:

Write several prepositions and/or prepositional phrases on the chalk board. The following words may be included:

above	between	on top of
along	by	over
at	down	through
behind	from	under
below	in the middle	underneath
beneath	on	upon
beside	on the bottom	within

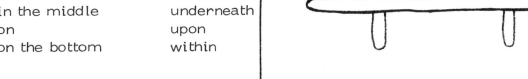

The vase is on the shelf.

Procedure:

A. Students may cut out and mount catalog pictures containing several items and write sentences using prepositions or phrases which correctly describe relative positions of the items in each picture.

B. Completed pages may be assembled in booklets for display.

Extension:

A. Students might select one catalog description and identify the prepositions in it.

B. Students might be assigned the task of writing sentences which contain a given number of prepositions. Example: Five sentences which contain one preposition.

THE WHOLE THING

Preparation:

A. Select a large catalog picture which illustrates a full-length person. Mount the picture on heavy paper, leaving writing space around the picture.

B. Draw lines to various parts of the anatomy such as the elbow, nose, ankle, foot, hip, wrist, lips, shoulder, etc. Number the lines.

Procedure:

A. Display the picture in a location where all students may have easy access to it while engaging in the activity.

B. Direct students to identify and correctly spell on separate paper each of the numbered body parts. Dictionaries may be used.

Extension:

A. As reinforcement, names of anatomy parts might be included in a spelling lesson.

B. A game might be played in which names of body parts might be written on small pieces of paper and placed in a grab-bag. Students might select a name and match the name with the correct body part on the picture.

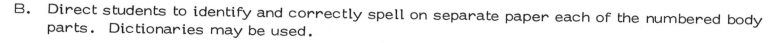

SENTENCE SENSE

Preparation:

Prepare on a spirit master, instructions for writing sentences which describe a catalog item.

Examples: A sentence which has one pronoun, one noun, and one verb.
A sentence which has one pronoun, one noun, one verb, and two adverbs.
A sentence which has two nouns, one verb, one adverb, one adjective, and one preposition.
A sentence which has one exclamatory word, two nouns, one verb, and two adverbs.
A sentence which has one adjective, one noun, and one verb.

Procedure:

A. Distribute a copy of the sentence building instructions to each student.

B. Direct students to cut out and mount on cards a quantity of item pictures equal to the number of sentence instructions written on the spirit master.

The candle is burning.

C. Students should then follow instructions for completing each sentence and write it below the appropriate picture.

Extension:

A. A game might be played where students might search their catalogs for words which represent given parts of speech.

39

B. Words in a catalog description might be scrambled and given to students. They might unscramble the words and write a sensible description.

SENTENCE SHAKE-UP

Preparation:

> Cut twelve large pictures of single items from the catalog and mount them on large sheets of paper. Around each picture list words which could be used in a sentence to describe the item in the picture.

the   as   is   cooking

pan   good

food   box   yellow

Procedure:

Display one picture with its corresponding words and direct students to use all words in making a sentence which would correctly describe the pictured item. Continue this for each of the twelve pictures.

PICTURE BOOK MAKERS

Preparation:

Create an atmosphere in which students
may pretend to be working for a
publishing firm in business for writing
books. A contest may be conducted
for selecting a name for the students'
book company.

Procedure:

A. Direct each student to prepare a
booklet of twenty—six blank pages
and a front cover. Each page
should be labeled at the top with
a letter of the alphabet.

B. Direct students to collect catalog
pictures of single items and mount
each on the appropriate page.

C. Books may be displayed where
other students might read and
evaluate them.

Extension:

Students might write short sentences about selected items in their booklets. (Nonreaders might
dictate sentences to the teacher.)

Preparation:

A. Prepare two picture cards per student. A picture of one item may be mounted on a small card with a wide left margin.

B. An appropriate modifying word may be written in the left margin.

C. Prepare the same number of verb and/or verb phrase cards. Be sure that each picture has a corresponding verb card that would complete a sentence when both are placed together.

Procedure:

A. Scatter cards over a table top or on the floor in an out-of-the-way location.

B. Explain that each student may select one picture card and one verb card which when read together would make a correct sentence.

C. Arrange classroom furniture in a long row with students facing each other. This will be Sentence Street.

Extension:

This might be conducted as an independent activity in which each student might write sentences using the matched cards.

Preparation:

    A.   Students may cut out pictures of single catalog items and mount them on cards.

    B.   The teacher writes below each picture a sentence which describes the item. One key word in the sentence may be underlined; this will be the word for which other synonyms may be substituted.

        Example: The window is <u>clean</u> and shiny.

Procedure:

    A.   Each student may obtain one picture-sentence card from the teacher.

    B.   He then chooses another word which means the same as the underlined word and rewrites the sentence with this new word.

Extension:

    Students might collect pictures of items which may be described by the same synonyms.

        Examples: The (door) fits well.
                         The (hat) fits well.
                         The (shoe) fits well.

ALPHA-BUILDERS

Preparation:

A. Determine the alphabetical sequence that is to be studied during the activity. (You may wish to use A-B-C-D-E or any other, such as K-L-M-N-O.) The activity may be repeated until the complete alphabet is studied.

B. Draw a large outline of a building on the chalk board. This will be the Alphabet Building. Label it with the letter sequence which is to be studied.

Procedure:

A. Direct students to select and read any catalog description. They may circle the first letter of the selected sequence as they read. The remaining sequence letters may be read and circled in the same way.

B. Students may write words containing the sequence letters on the alphabet building. These may be read to the class.

Alphabet House

A - B - C - D

at   by   can

unbreakable   do   done

Extension:

Students might alphabetize all words in their descriptions.

44

Preparation:

A. Each student may cut out three pictures
    of single items and mount them on a page.
    Below each picture he should write one
    sentence which describes the item.

B. Completed pages are handed to the
    teacher who underlines one descriptive
    word in each sentence and returns
    the papers to the student.

Procedure:

A. Direct students to rewrite the
    sentences using a word opposite
    in meaning to the word underlined.

B. Students may read both the original
    sentence and the new sentence to the
    class.

C. A follow-up discussion will clarify the meaning of the word antonym and its use in writing.

Extension:

A. A duplicated work sheet might be prepared listing words from the catalog. Students might
    write antonyms for each word.

B. Students might construct their own file of words with corresponding antonyms. These
    might be exchanged and read by other students.

Sailing on the lake is fun.

Preparation:

Prepare a spirit master of the alphabet, leaving a blank space after each letter. Distribute a copy to each student.

Procedure:

Students may select words from their catalogs and write the words in the appropriate blanks.

Extension:

A. Word lists to be alphabetized by students might be selected from a catalog index. These lists might consist of words which represent the complete alphabet or be restricted to words which begin with the same letter.

B. Pictures might be substituted for item names in completing each sequence.

Word Order		
A Arrow	N	
B	O	
C	P	
D	Q	
E	R	

SPELLER TELLERS

Preparation:

    Small cards or the equivalent may be used by each student in constructing word banks.

Procedure:

A. Students may pretend to be tellers in charge of individual word banks. The bank may consist of a small box or envelope in which word deposits may be made. (Students may wish to apply special "wordy" decorations to their banks.)

B.   Each student may select from the catalog words which he or she wishes to learn to spell each week. Selections may be written on cards and deposited in the individual's bank.

C.   Students may choose partners for listening to each other's spelling.

Preparation:

A collection of item descriptions should be cut from the catalog. These descriptions will be read to students who may tell the meanings of selected words. The word meanings should be unknown to the students so that context clues might be used. Interest will be added by preparing some type of award hat which may be worn by the game's winner each day.

> Oval Pool Outfit – Three-feet-deep pool has unique oval shape that fits into smaller spaces but still provides ample swimming area.

Procedure:

Explain how the game will be played. One item description will be read and individuals will be directed to tell the meaning of selected words. The daily winner will get to wear the award hat for that day.

Example of questions from description above:

1. What is the meaning of unique?
2. What is the meaning of ample?
3. What is the meaning of oval?

Extension:

Each student might construct a word bank of new words learned from the game. These collections might be checked periodically to determine how the student's vocabulary has progressed.

WORD POWER

Preparation:

Select several item descriptions from the catalog and write them on a spirit master. Above each description, write the name of the item.

Single-Speed Boy's Bike

Red finished tubular-steel frame with handsome black overspray. 20 x 1.75 inch black knobby tires. Low cross-braced, black handlebars. Padded "dirt-bike" saddle styling.

Procedure:

Distribute the duplicated descriptions. Direct students to read each description and underline words which precisely describe the item. (Examples from the above description: <u>red</u>, <u>knobby</u>, <u>cross-braced</u>, <u>padded</u>, and <u>black</u>.

GIVE THE WORD

Preparation:

A. Cut out and mount several pictures of single catalog items on heavy paper.

B. Compose sentences which may be completed with the name of a pictured item. These
sentences may be read to the students.

Procedure:

A. Select four or five students for participation
in this activity. The activity may be repeated
until every student participates.

B. Display mounted pictures where students
may easily view them.

C. Explain that names of pictured items may
be used in completing the sentences read
by the teacher. Students may take turns
responding to the sentences. Sentence
examples for the mounted pictures shown
could be:

1. To pound nails we use a _____ .
2. A _____ is used to make pictures.
3. We wear _____ to keep our feet warm.
4. A _____ usually has four legs.
5. Skates have _____ wheels.

Context Clues
Intermediate Level

COPY WRITERS

Preparation:

Prepare on a spirit master a list of specialized words which would be used in writing a
description of a particular catalog item (three different items). The words should be

50

listed below the name of the item. Each student should receive a copy of these words.
Examples are:

Boat	Dress	Television
fiberglass	silk	brown
hull	belted	early–American
sleek	flare	cabinet
anchor	pleated	25–inch
blue	attractive	glass
windshield	red	hidden
galley		controls

Procedure:

A. Word lists may be given to the students. Direct them to use the words to write a description
of the items listed. Other words may be used, but those in each list must be used
in the new description.

B. Each description should be written on a separate page with room at the top for an illustration
of the item being described. (Students must take care that the pictured item corresponds
to the written description.)

C. Illustrated pages with descriptions may be assembled into miniature catalogs for display.

Extension:

Individual cards with item pictures and lists of correct and incorrect descriptive words might be
prepared. Students might then select the words from the list which would describe the pictured
item.

MATCH AND ATTACH

Preparation:

A. Cut out twelve pictures of single catalog items and mount them on cards. Paste the catalog descriptions of these items on separate cards. Number the picture cards and letter the description cards. (Do in random order so as not to provide clues as to how the cards would match.)

B. Prepare an answer key showing the correct matches of pictures and descriptions. Place materials in an envelope and label "Match and Attach".

Procedure:

Students may pair each pictured item with its matching description and use the answer key for self-evaluation.

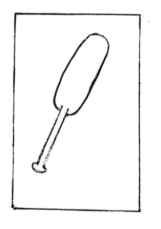

A.
made with
varnished
quality
hardware
for speed

PICTURE CUES

Preparation:

A. Cut twelve large pictures of single items from the catalog and mount them on heavy paper. Write the item's name above the picture.

B. Prepare a dittoed work sheet containing ten sentences, each of which has one word omitted. (This missing word must be the name of one of the twelve pictured items.) Where the word is omitted in the sentence, enter the same number of dashes as there are letters in the omitted word.

1. The _ _ _ _ is pretty.
2. This is my new _ _ _ _ .
3. My new _ _ _ _ _ are red.
4. The _ _ _ _ _ has six buttons.
5. The _ _ _ _ _ _ is soft.

Procedure:

A. Display the twelve pictures where all students may see them and distribute the duplicated work sheets to the students.

B. Explain that each sentence has a missing word which is the name of one of the pictured items.

C. Direct students to fill in the blank spaces with the correct words.

Extension:

Students might prepare their own puzzle sentences and then ask other students to supply the omitted word.

Preparation:

Select an item description which all students are able to read and comprehend. If all catalogs are alike, the same description may be used by every student. If not, then different descriptions will have to be used. This exercise will provide experience in recognizing how certain words control a paragraph's meaning.

Procedure:

A. Create an atmosphere in which the students may pretend to be catalog editors who have the power to change any written material in the catalog.

B. Either the teacher or a student may read aloud the selected item's description.

C. Direct each student to completely change the description's meaning by changing any of the words and rewriting the description.

D. Each student may read his or her revised description to the class. The class may decide whether the meaning is sufficiently changed.

Extension:

A. Students might be grouped in pairs whereby one student writes a short paragraph favorable to some selected item while the other student writes a paragraph unfavorable to the item. These might be read to the class.

B. The activity might be extended to include newspaper paragraph changes. Each student might make key changes which would change a selected paragraph's meaning.

C. Students might rewrite a selected paragraph by using synonyms which would retain the original meaning.

FINDERS KEEPERS

Preparation:

A. Cut out twenty-four pictures of single items and mount each on a card. Write the item's name below the picture but omit key vowel(s). Number each card for later use in evaluation. Place cards in an envelope labeled "Finders Keepers".

B. Write the item's complete name on the reverse side of each card. Students may use these for self-evaluation.

Procedure:

A. Explain how the materials are to be used. Each student may do the activity in his or her free time. The name of each item may be completed by supplying the missing vowel(s).

B. Caution students not to mark on any of the cards. Answers may be written on a separate sheet of paper, using the number on the cards. (If a laminating machine is available, the cards may be laminated so answers may be written directly on the cards.)

Extension:

A. Another set of picture cards might display a single item with two words on each card. Only one word would correctly spell the name of the pictured item.

B. Charts might be prepared with a word bank of item names at the top and pictures of the items below. The correct item name would be selected from the word bank.

MENTAL MAGIC

Preparation:

    Assemble a collection of pictures and descriptions of items. Each description should contain familiar words so that students might easily form mental images from hearing the description.

Procedure:

A. Direct the students to listen as an item's description is read and then draw a picture of the item described.

B. Direct students to tell what they believe the item is and show the drawn pictures.

WHAT IS THIS?

Polished aluminum legs. Blue nylon mesh on sides. Plastic pad over hardboard floor. Wheels on two legs.

C. The actual picture may be presented after all students have responded. Classmates may determine which student's selection (drawing) is most accurate. An award badge may be given to each winner.

Structural Analysis
Intermediate Level

DOUBLE WACKERS, WORD CRACKERS

Preparation:

A. Students should have had experiences with consonants, vowels, word syllables, and dictionary usage before engaging in this activity.

B. Prepare a list of catalog words containing double letters.

Procedure:

A. Draw a large anvil with two giant hammers posed over it on the chalkboard (or large sheet of mural paper).

B. Explain that a special catalog word will be written, but not read, on the anvil space. (Words will be special because they contain double letters.) Direct the student to copy the word on paper and use the dictionary to find out how the word could be divided into syllables. The first student who writes the word on the anvil drawing and correctly tells how it could be divided wins the game.

57

CATCH A COMPOUND

Preparation:

A. This is a game activity.

B. Divide students into three or four teams. Students may select a name for their team and elect a team manager.

Procedure:

A. Each team member selects a catalog page and records on paper all the compound words he can find on that page.

B. Team managers tally their team's total words. The winner will be the team which finds the most compound words.

Extension:

A. A given description might be rewritten without using the compound words which the original description contained. Rewritten descriptions might be read aloud.

B. Students might use catalog pictures to illustrate a booklet of compound words.

WHOSE IS IT?

Preparation:

None

Procedure:

A. Direct students to cut out and mount ten pictures of catalog items on writing paper. Students may then write one sentence using some possessive form for describing each item.

B. Invite each student to show a picture and read the sentence.

C. Display pages of completed sentences around the room in order that all students may read them.

Extension:

A. The activity may be broadened to include possessive pronouns (without an apostrophe).

B. Students may count the times possessive forms are used in a given item description.

C. A list of catalog words may be dittoed; then students are asked to write the possessive form of each word. Some examples of catalog words are:

| clock | game | train | radio |
| football | men | bag | table |

CONTACTING CONTRACTIONS

Preparation:

    A.   Provide dictionaries to be used to determine root words.

    B.   Create a communications station by drawing a building with a large antenna on the chalk board or mural paper.

Procedure:

    A.   Students may select any item description and identify word contractions contained in the description.

    B.   Write contractions and root words as if radiating from the antenna.

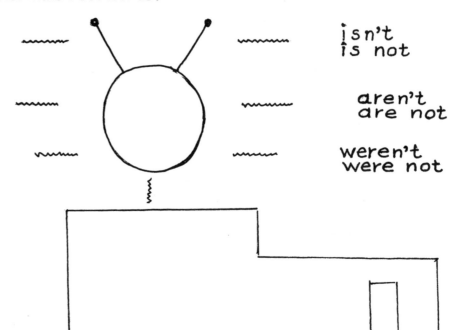

isn't
is not

aren't
are not

weren't
were not

Extension:

    A.   A game may be played between two students in which one student gives a contraction and the second student gives the root words.

    B.   Students may count and record the number of times contractions are used on a given catalog page.

    C.   Students may use contractions in writing sentence captions for selected catalog pictures.

Preparation:

A. Cut out and mount twelve pictures of familiar catalog items on large cards. Below each picture, write the same number of blank lines as there are letters in the item's name. Write the item's name on the back side of the card.

B. Write four complete alphabets on one-half inch square pieces of heavy paper. Place these in a small paper bag or similar container.

Procedure:

A. This game is for two players.

B. Each player may take one picture card. Turns may be taken to select letters from the grab bag in an attempt to spell the name of the pictured item. Unused letters may be returned to the grab bag. The winner will be the first student who correctly spells the item's name. (Answers may be checked by reading the correct name on the back of each card.)

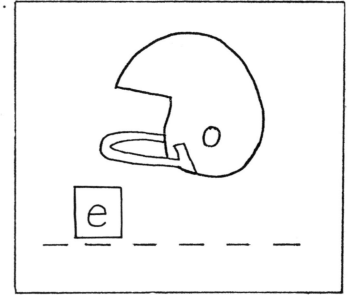

C. New picture cards may be selected for each new game.

Extension:

Students may search for additional pictures of items whose names might be spelled with letters from the grab bag.

Preparation:

A. Select three or four random catalog descriptions which contain words with prefixes and/or suffixes and copy the descriptions on a spirit master.

B. Direct students to cut the shape of a garden spade from paper.

Procedure:

A. Explain that students may use the spades to "dig out" root words.

B. Distribute copies of the catalog descriptions. Direct them to read each description and list the words which contain prefixes and/or suffixes and write the root words on the spade.

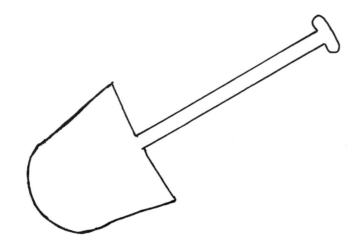

return - turn

shirts - shirt

C. Direct students to tape their spades of words to the chalk board for all to read.

D. Students may ask a friend to cover his or her spade with a piece of paper while he or she spells the root words that have been "dug out".

Extension:

Several prefixes and suffixes may be written on the chalk board for students to use in writing sentences.

Preparation:

A. Copy several catalog descriptions on a spirit master. (Select those which contain several prepositional phrases.)

B. Draw a large penguin on the chalk board paper. Write the words, "Preppie Penguin (Leave writing space to the right of the

or on a large sheet of mural says," above the picture. picture.)

Procedure:

A. Place students in two teams for playing the game.

B. Distribute a copy of the catalog descriptions to each student. Direct each to read the descriptions and underline prepositional phrases. (Students may not exchange answers before or during the game.)

C. Direct one student to select one prepositional phrase used in a description and write the phrase next to the "Preppie Penguin". A student from the second team may then go to the drawing and write a sentence using the prepositional phrase. If both answers are correct, both teams receive a point. An incorrect answer does not receive a point.

D. Alternate the teams in writing phrases and sentences. The team with the most points at the end of a predetermined time wins the game.

Preparation:

Provide dictionaries to be used for correctly spelling the original words.
Examples of catalog abbreviations are:

shpg.	yd.	UL
wt.	incl.	dk
oz.	dia.	reg.
in.	v.	med.
A.C.	ctn.	sm.

Procedure:

A. Direct students to read catalog descriptions and note any abbreviations used. Then with dictionaries, they may write the original form of each abbreviation.

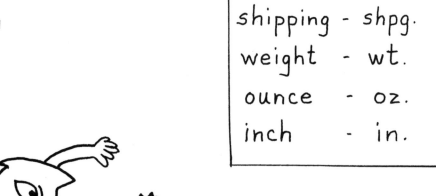

shipping - shpg.
weight - wt.
ounce - oz.
inch - in.

B. Direct students to write the abbreviated and original words on a class chart.

Extension:

A. Students may list abbreviations from sources other than catalogs.

B. A game may be played where students try listing the most abbreviations within a given period of time.

SUPER SYLLABLES

Preparation:

Draw a picture of a house with at least four floor levels on the chalk board. The first floor may be designated the first floor for one-syllable words, second floor for two-syllable words, the third floor for three-syllable words, and the fourth floor for four-syllable words. (Leave plenty of writing space at each floor level.)

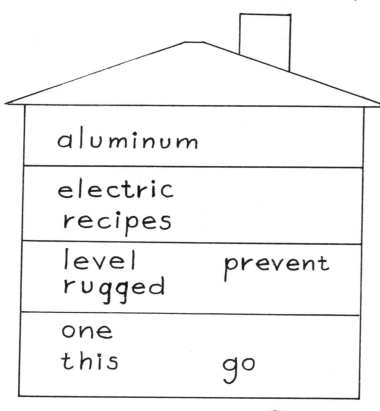

aluminum

electric
recipes

level   prevent
rugged

one
this   go

Procedure:

Invite students to help build the syllable house by searching catalogs for words containing one, two, three, and four syllables and writing the words on the appropriate floor level. (The more words, the sturdier the house!)

Extension:

A. Students may maintain their own syllable house booklets to be exchanged and read by other students.

B. Students may write stories using words of a given syllable number, i.e., words of only one syllable, words of only two syllables, etc.

65

Preparation:

A.   Cut thirty or forty pictures of single items from the catalog and mount the pictures on heavy paper.

B.   Draw a large scoreboard on the chalk board where team scores may be posted during the game.

Procedure:

Team 1	Team 2

A.   Divide the class into teams. Show one picture to the class and ask for either the beginning or final sound in the item's name. The student who gives the correct answer gets to keep the picture and a point is registered on the scoreboard for his team.

B.   Try to give every student equal opportunity for answering. The team scoring the most points wins the game.

Extension:

A.   Students might collect other pictures of items which match the beginning and final sounds of given pictured items.

B.   Students might use the pictured item's name in a sentence after the beginning and final sounds have been given.

UP THE LADDER--WITH VOWELS

Preparation:

A ladder–type structure of paper
is required for each student in
this activity. A ladder may be drawn
on five sheets of writing paper which
are stapled together along the vertical
edges. This will provide a ladder
about four feet long. (A ladder may
also be constructed from cardboard.)

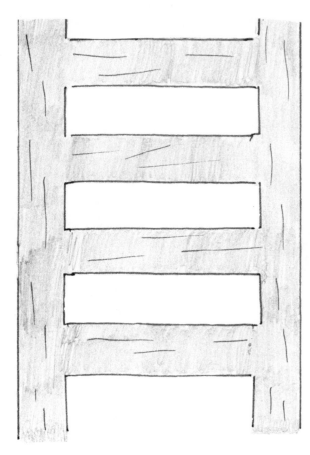

Procedure:

A. Provide or assist each student in
constructing a ladder similar to
the above.

B. Direct students to search catalog
descriptions for words which contain
a given number of vowels. The
bottom ladder rung may be used
for recording words which contain
only one vowel, the second rung for
words with two vowels, etc.

C. Each rung may have a minimum of three recorded words before the student "climbs" to the
next rung.

Extension:

The ladder structure might be used for collecting other words, i.e., parts of speech, double
words, words with specific consonants, etc.

Preparation:

None

Procedure:

Begin the activity by saying, "Let's travel to (the selected area)." Then direct students to collect pictures of items whose names begin with the same letter as the initial letter in the location's name. Pictures may be cut out and placed in an envelope bearing the name of the selected location or they may be pasted on sheets of paper labeled with the location's name.

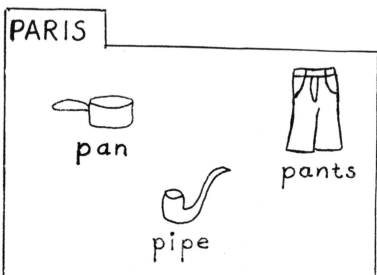

PARIS

pan

pants

pipe

Extension:

Pictures of items found at a given location might be pasted in an alphabetized sequence to large sheets of paper, i.e., items found in a store, office, etc.

VIVID VOWELS

Preparation:

A. For this activity students may be grouped in five picture-collecting teams. Each team may be assigned one vowel letter.

B. One student from each team may be elected to wear that team's "vowel coat" on which the team members may paste pictures of items whose names begin with the assigned vowel.

C. A paper vowel coat may be easily constructed by cutting two pieces of mural paper long enough to cover the student from neck to ankles and stapling the two pieces along the vertical edges. The wearer of the coat may be assigned the task of decorating a special hat to wear during the activity. The hat would identify the assigned vowel.

Procedure:

A. Team members find pictures and paste them on their team's coat, i.e., the a team would paste only items beginning with the vowel a to their coat. Encourage students to be creative in outfitting their coats with pictures.

B. The finished coat of each team may be evaluated by other team members. All pictured item names must begin with the assigned vowel.

Preparation:

An atmosphere may be created in which students may pretend to be detectives searching for a given consonant blend. Assign several students to a detective team and assign a different blend to each team, i.e., one team may search for the st blend, another the cr blend, another the dr blend, etc.

Procedure:

A. Direct team members to count the number of times their assigned blend appears on a given catalog page.

B. As each student detective determines the frequency of his or her assigned blend, that number may be written on the chalk board. (Individual team frequencies may vary because of differences in student abilities.) An average of counts by each team may indicate which blend is most often used.

Extension:

A. Students might read the same catalog description for determining the number of times a given consonant blend appears.

B. Students might determine which consonant blend appears most often and which appears least often in a given catalog description.

St	Cr	Dr	Bl	
John-4	Joe-3	Bill-4	Lee-4	
Sue-3	Vic-5	Greg-5	Jill-6	
Si -6	Jo-4	Jim-3	Sam-3	
Avg. 4	Avg. 4	Avg-4	Avg. 4	

Preparation:

    A. Draw a picture of a food blender on a large sheet of mural paper. Attach a small paper bag and tape the drawing to the wall where students may easily reach into the bag.

    B. Write the following consonant blends on twenty-two small one-inch square pieces of paper. Place these in the bag.

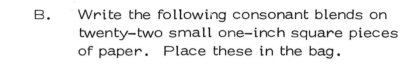

bl	dr	gl	sc	sn	tr
br	dw	gr	sk	sp	tw
cl	fl	pl	sl	st	
cr	fr	pr	sm	sw	

Procedure:

    A. Direct each student to select one blend card from the blender bag. After recording the blend, the student may return the card to the bag and the next student may select a card.

    B. Direct students to collect pictures of items whose names begin with the same consonant blend as that selected from the blender bag and paste them on a piece of paper.

Preparation:

A.   Cut twelve pictures of individual items from the catalog and glue each on a separate page. Include items both familiar and unfamiliar to the students. Number each page for identification purposes.

B.   Write next to each picture an incomplete sentence which asks why an item is needed. Use a variety of sentence forms such as, "I am needed for...," "I may be used for...," "My function is...," or "I am most popularly used as...."

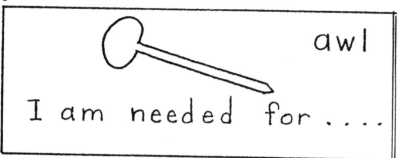

Procedure:

Direct students to complete the sentence on each picture card.

Extension:

A.   Students may collect item pictures for use in writing sentences which begin "Without this, there would be no ...."

B.   Students may list items in their classroom which could be removed without jeopardizing daily functions.

Preparation:

A. Direct each student to cut out a picture of a single item and paste it on a sheet of paper. (Space should be left below each picture for additional written statements.) Each student should write his or her name on the paper before handing it to the teacher.

B. Write in the space below the picture several factual and several opinionated statements which refer to the item.

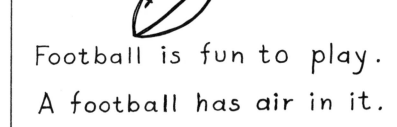

David

Football is fun to play.

A football has air in it.

Procedure:

A. Return each picture to the appropriate student.

B. Direct students to silently read their statements and mark whether each statement is fact or opinion.

C. Ask each student to read aloud his or her responses to the statements.

Extension:

A. Students may read magazine advertisements and decide which statements are factual.

B. Students may observe a given situation, i.e., a basketball game, a grocery shopper, etc., and record some observed facts and some opinions about the situation. These may be read aloud.

Preparation:

Write the following categories and budget allowances on the chalk board.

Furniture $600   Hardware $90

Sports $150   Books $75

Clothing $100   Toys $65

Procedure:

A. Direct students to work in pairs for this activity.

B. Allot a specific amount of money for each pair of "budget makers.

C. Direct students to copy the item categories on their papers. (Writing space should be left below each heading.) Students may then select items for pretend purchases in each category without going over the allotted money. Names and prices of selected items may be written below each major heading and prices totaled for each category.

D. Completed budget sheets may be exchanged with companion "budget markers" for checking.

MISSING ITEM EXPERTS

Preparation:

A.   Play this game with the total class.

B.   Cut out and paste twenty-four large pictures on heavy paper. (Students may do this.) Each picture should illustrate several items.

C.   Construct paper badge awards for game winners.

Procedure:

A.   Students may observe as three pictures are presented by the teacher. After a minute or so, the teacher may turn away from the class and remove one picture and again present the remaining pictures.

B.   Students may take turns identifying items in the missing picture. A student who correctly identifies all items in the missing picture will win the game and be declared a "Missing Item Expert".

Extension:

A.   Recorded sound collections may be substituted for picture collections. Students may then identify missing sounds.

B.   Students may go on an "item" walk. After returning to the classroom, they may tell what and where different items were located.

ANSWERING SERVICE

Critical Thinking
Intermediate Level

Preparation:

A. Cut out twelve catalog descriptions and paste each to a large card, leaving space below for several questions. Number each card for identification.

B. Write several questions relating to the description on each card. Some questions may be answered directly from the descriptive information while others may be answered only through inference. Prepare an answer key for the questions on each card. Place cards in an envelope.

> 1. Blocks of fun shapes and colors. Develops balance skills. Smooth edges come in six colors. Fit in a plastic bag for storage.
>
> 1. Are the blocks made from wood?
> 2. How many colors are available?
> 3. How could the blocks be used?

Procedure:

A. Present the materials to the class. Direct students to read the cards and answer the questions in their free time.

B. Direct students to use the answer keys to evaluate their completed work.

Extension:

Students may develop their own questions regarding a selected description and ask other students to respond to these questions.

SAME BUT DIFFERENT

Preparation:

Direct each student to cut out two different pictures of the same item, i.e., two different coffee pots, two different bicycles, etc. These pictures may be mounted on writing paper.

Procedure:

Direct each student to write below the mounted pictures how the items are different and how they are alike. These lists may be read to the class.

Extension:

A. Students may compare and contrast two classmates and tell why it's good that they are not exactly alike.

B. Students may survey the classroom and record items which are alike and different.

1. Both pots have handles.
2. They both have lids.
3. The pots are not the same size.

Preparation:

A. Direct each student to cut out and paste one picture of any single item to a card which may be used as a computation card. The actual price of the item may be written above the picture. Cards may then be handed to the teacher who may write below the picture an amount of money which the student may pay for the purchase, i.e., one dollar, five dollars, ten dollars, etc. (The amount should be greater than the actual cost of the item.)

B. Draw or paint a cashier's window on a large sheet of paper and label it "The Money Changer". Paste an envelope to the bottom of the drawing to be used for student deposits.

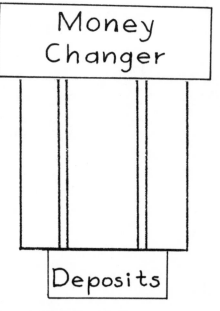

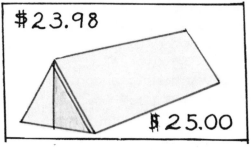

$23.98

$25.00

Procedure:

A. Distribute one item picture to each student. Direct each student to compute the amount of money returned when purchasing that particular item. (Dollar values written on each card may be used in the transaction.)

B. Direct students to deposit their computation cards in the envelope on the cashier's window to be evaluated by the "head cashier" (the teacher or a designated student).

Extension:

A play store may be created where students may purchase items (pictures) with play money.
A follow-up trip to a real store may be taken in order that students may make nominal purchases.

Preparation:

Select a panel of three students who may decide which game-player makes the most logical item selections in the game.

Procedure:

A. Students may select, within five minute periods, any three items for pretended purchase from the catalog.

B. Each item's name, and reasons for its purchase, may be written on paper to be read aloud at the end of the period.

C. The judgment panel, after listening to all reasons, may select the most logical purchase. Judges may also give reasons for their selections.

Extension:

A. Students may go on a field trip to a local store where they may compare costs and qualities of several similar items. They may decide which would be the best purchase.

B. A class debate may be conducted with respect to whether a particular catalog item merits purchase. The class may be divided; those for purchase and those against purchase.

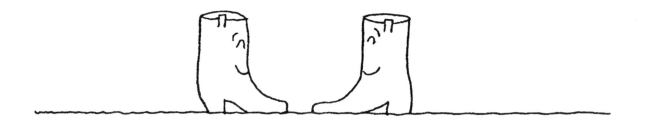

Preparation:

A. Select ten large pictures of single items illustrated in a catalog identical to those of several students. Record the page number of each picture. (Don't cut out the pictures.)

B. For each picture, prepare several true-false statements which refer to the item to be read to the students.

   Example: (Page 31, Top Picture)

      1. Back darts to provide poor fit.   True   False
      2. Button and tie back closing.   True   False
      3. Shipping weight 6 ounces.   True   False

C. For a game board, draw a large rectangle on the chalk board and divide it into twenty-one vertical sections. (One section may be labeled the starting position, ten sections labeled winning positions, and ten sections labeled losing positions.)

Procedure:

A. Place students in two teams. Ensure that each student is near a catalog which contains the selected pictures.

B. Explain that both teams may be positioned (by written marks) at the starting position on the game board. Statements will be read which require a true or false answer. Correct answers may move a team toward the winner's position (one space at a time) while incorrect answers may move a team toward the loser's position (one space at a time). A team may become the winner by being the first across the winner's end or if the opposing team moves across the loser's end. Each student may take a turn at answering a question.

TAKE IT APART

Preparation:

None

Procedure:

A. Direct students to select and cut out one picture of a single item. (The description need not be included.) The item should consist of several moving parts, such as watch, bicycle, typewriter, gym set, microscope, recorders, etc.

B. Direct students to list (write) the names of the various parts which make up each item.

C. Each student may present his or her picture and read the recorded parts of each item to the class.

Extension:

A. Students may tell what could happen to their items if given parts were missing.

B. Names of item parts may be used in a spelling lesson. Each student may contribute names from his or her item for this lesson.

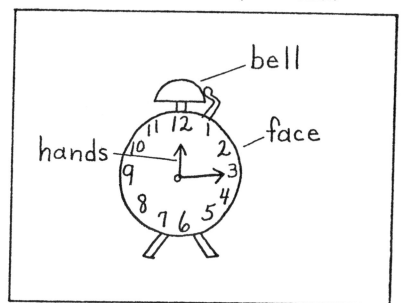

Preparation:

   A.   Cut several pieces of heavy cardboard to fit normal picture frames. These pieces should
        be identical in measurements as the catalogs' available picture frames. Examples: 3 x 5",
        5 x 7", 8 x 10", 11 x 14", 16 x 20", etc.

   B.   Glue a full-size picture on each cardboard. Number the cardboard pictures and place them
        in a large envelope. These numbers may be used in constructing an answer key.

Procedure:

   A.   Present materials (cardboard pictures) to the students with an explanation that this is a free
        time activity.

   B.   Students may obtain the materials and measure each piece of cardboard for the purpose
        of ordering a frame. Measurements may be checked against the answer key. Order forms
        in the catalog may be used or students may design their own.

Extension:

   A.   Students may cut additional pictures from catalogs and frame the pictures with cardboard.

   B.   Students may design and decorate colorful cardboard frames for use in displaying creative
        stories which students might write on any subject. Stories might be exchanged and read
        by other students.

SIZE SELECTIONS

Preparation:

A. Most large catalogs have a clothing size chart located near the index pages. Provide one of these charts.

B. Mount five pictures and corresponding descriptions of clothing items on cards. Number each item.

C. Below each picture, write a question asking the size needed for a given student. (Questions may be answered with the chart.) Place materials in an envelope and prepare an answer key.

 What size robe for a girl 48 inches tall?

 What size jeans for a boy who weighs 65 pounds and is 55 inches tall?

Procedure:

A. Students may read the questions below the descriptions and then determine the required sizes by using size charts.

B. Students may use the answer key to self-evaluate their work.

Extension:

Students might use their own physical measurements to determine required clothing sizes.

WORD STRETCHERS

Preparation:

A. Discuss with students how catalog descriptions are sprinkled with many descriptive words, some of which seem almost to exaggerate values of particular items.

B. Draw on the chalk board a large rubber band, making it appear as though it is being stretched. Write in its center the words "Word Stretchers".

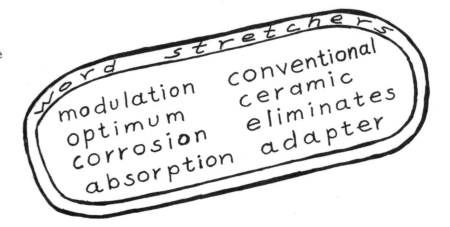

Procedure:

A. Students may read several catalog descriptions and write within the rubber band space any unusual words used to describe an item. This may be continued until twelve or fifteen words have been listed.

B. Students may find meanings of the unusual words in a dictionary. Word meanings may be recorded and used in a class discussion on how catalog descriptions are sometimes slanted with superlatives.

Extension:

Students may cut out one pictured item and then write a description of it using only superlatives. Descriptions may be compiled in Superlative Booklets and displayed where students may read them.

HISTORY OF ME

Preparation:

Dictionaries and encyclopedias should be accessible.

Procedure:

A. Introduce the activity by focusing student attention on selected item(s). An electric iron may be used. What if the iron could speak? Could it tell an interesting story of its history?

B. Direct students to create "History of Me" booklets. The history would relate to a personified catalog item and not to the student. Each student may select pictures of catalog items and paste each near the top of a page. Pertinent information about each item found in reference books may be written below the picture.

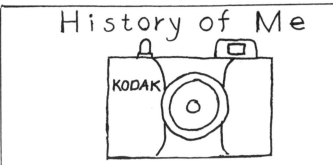

Extension:

A. A booklet of personal history may be written by each student. These biographies may be exchanged and read by classmates.

B. Reference books may be used to compile lists of facts about given items, i.e., facts about smoking, facts about gardening, etc.

Preparation:

A. Prepare dittoed copies of simulated mailing envelopes and stamps by ruling a spirit master into thirds. Write on each envelope several questions which require a parcel post chart for answering.

> 1. How much to send 20 pounds to zone 3?
>
> S m i l e

B. A simulated mail box may be constructed from a shoe box, painted red, white, and blue, and labeled "mail box".

Procedure:

A. Distribute envelopes and direct students to use parcel post charts in their catalogs to find answers for the questions.

Red

Blue

Mail
Box

White

B. Direct students to deposit their completed envelopes in the mail box.

Extension:

Students may read about the history of the United States Postal Service and present oral reports about its development.

Preparation:

A prior discussion relating to the nature of local sales tax may be required before students may successfully work with this activity.

Procedure:

A. Direct each student to cut out pictures of ten items they would like to purchase. These pictures may be pasted on regular writing paper. The item's price may be written above each picture.

B. Direct the students to compute the actual amount of sales tax required when purchasing the item. The catalog's order forms should indicate just how much tax would be owed (what percentage).

C. The required tax and total cost of each item should be written below each picture.

$7.99

Tax _____

Total _____

Extension:

A. Students may read about various taxes, i.e., sales, income, personal, etc. Written reports may be prepared and read to the class.

B. Reference books may be consulted for determining how tax money is used. What would be some consequences if taxes were never paid? Oral reports may be presented.

WISHBOOKING

Preparation:

A. Each student should have a catalog order form for the activity. If student catalogs contain order forms, use those. If not, prepare an order form on a spirit master.

B. Students may require much individual assistance with their order preparations.

C. A mailbox (to be used for mailing completed orders) may be easily constructed from a shoe box painted red, white, and blue.

Procedure:

A. Students may pretend to be catalog shoppers. Distribute the duplicated order forms. (Or students may tear forms from their catalogs.)

B. The teacher may discuss and explain ordering procedures. (An example may be helpful to students.)

C. Students may order any two items they desire. Completed orders may be folded and deposited in the mailbox. The teacher or a student checker may read and evaluate each order.

Extension:

A. A monetary limit might be placed on orders. Students would then select items within a given budget.

B. Orders may be restricted to items used for special occasions, i.e., Easter clothes, camping trips, home remodeling, etc.

C. A distribution center may be established where some students would receive completed orders. These students may fill orders with pictures of items on each order form and return the items to the original shopper.

SEARCH AND READ

Preparation:

Students may be placed in two teams. The game may be expedited by using pre-selected
item names, i.e., camping equipment, kitchen appliances, wrenches, auto supplies, etc.

Procedure:

A.   The game plan may be explained to the two teams. The teacher may read the name of
some catalog item and each contestant may use the index in searching for the page on
which that item is located. The first contestant to find the item may read the item's
description; that team may receive a point.

B.   The game may end at a predetermined time. The team with the most points wins.

Extension:

A dittoed list of unfamiliar item names may be distributed to each student. The catalog's
index may be used to identify the items and to write a description of each.

ESP BAG

Preparation:

Select pictures of twenty single items from the catalog and paste them on individual cards.
Place these pictures in a large paper bag which has been decorated with magical doodles.

(Students should not see the mounted pictures at any time before the activity.)

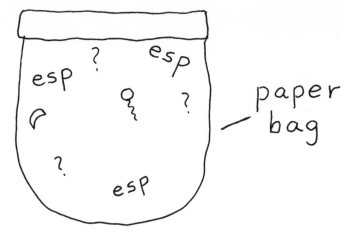

paper bag

Procedure:

A. Create an "ESP atmosphere" where students may pretend to be clairvoyants intent on describing unseen pictures of items. (Special "brain-wave hats" may be designed and worn by each student during the activity.)

B. Identify one student as the ESPer to begin the game. He or she may choose one picture from the bag. The picture may not be shown to other game contestants.

C. Direct students to take turns in asking questions which may lead to the identity of the pictured item held by the ESPer.

D. The game continues until all pictures have been identified.

Extension:

Students may write questions relating to the identity of an unknown item selected by the teacher. These questions may be exchanged and read by classmates.

Preparation:

A. Paint a "make believe" house on a large sheet of cardboard. The front should be large enough for a student to get behind and be out of sight from the class. Cut out one window of the house to display a toy picture.

B. Cut out and paste pictures of single toy items on cards. Prepare pictures so that each student may have one.

Procedure:

A. Each student may pretend a pictured toy item has come alive for the day and is speaking about its experiences.

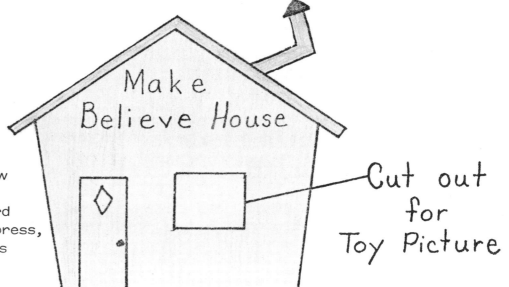

B. Each student may display the pictured toy in the cut-out window in the "make believe" house. While sitting behind the cardboard front, the student may orally express, in first person delivery, the toy's reaction to being alive.

Cut out for Toy Picture

Extension:

Students, while pretending to be the toy, may respond to questions asked by classmates.

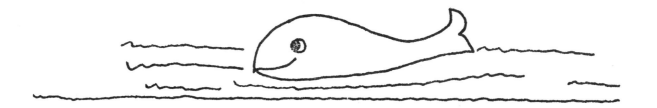

Preparation:

A. Direct students to cut out and mount on cardboard the head portions of large-size catalog models. Students may paste cardboard pieces to the backs of their mounted pictures so pictures will stand in upright positions. (Each student may prepare one fictional person.)

 Front ←   Back →

B. Create a nook for mind reading by fastening two long pieces of cardboard together along one edge. These may be placed in a vertical position behind a table.

Procedure:

A. Each student may take a turn in placing his or her mounted picture on the "mind reader's" table and then sitting behind the table.

B. Observing students may relay questions to the "mind reader", asking what the fictional person believes about given topics. Example: "What does the person think about our nation going to the metric system?"

CAREER DAY

Preparation:

Create a Career Information Banner by taping a long piece of mural paper to the chalk board or classroom wall.

Procedure:

A. Students may use their catalogs to select pictures which represent a career topic, i.e., typewriters for typists, music instruments for musicians, clothes for models, microscopes for scientists, etc.

B. Catalog pictures which relate to a selected topic may be cut out and pasted on the Career Banner. (The completed banner should illustrate a variety of career possibilities.)

C. Students may gather additional information about their chosen careers from other references and organize the information for an oral report.

D. Each student may tell the class about his or her career selection.

Extension:

Community people who represent various career possibilities may be invited to visit the class for a speaker-student exchange.

Preparation:

A. Prepare a list of catalog items. (Students should not see this list.) The number of items should equal the number of students who may engage in the activity.

B. Direct students to create a "game show format" on either the chalk board or on mural paper. Students may draw and/or paint a typical stage setting to be used as the backdrop of this activity.

Procedure:

A. Three students may be selected to begin the activity. Standing before the class and in front of the backdrop, each student may select one of three item choices read aloud by the teacher. The student should tell why that particular item was chosen over the other two items.

B. The best speech of the three students may be determined by directing the class to applaud for the student who presented the best speech. (The winning student would be the one with the most applause.)

C. These procedures may be continued until all students have participated.

Extension:

Students may be directed to a given catalog page. One student may be assigned a given item and directed to tell how that item could be used.

SENTIMENTAL JOURNEY

Preparation:

A. Students may create mock travel cases in which to "pack" pictures of selected items for the trip. The travel cases may be as simple as two sheets of paper stapled along three edges or as elaborate as a cardboard box.

B. Students may create a mock depot siding by painting a colorful building front on a large piece of cardboard.

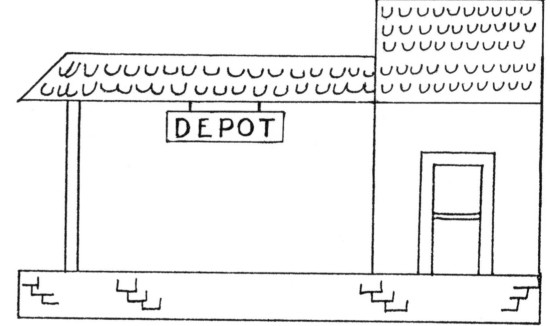

Procedure:

A. Each student may decide where he or she would like to go and then select items for that trip. Pictures of items may be cut out and packed in individual travel cases.

B. Each student may take a turn standing before the depot and telling where he or she plans to go. The student may take each item from the travel case and tell why it was selected for the trip. (The travel case and items may be taped to the side of the depot for display after each trip is explained.)

Extension:

Students may be encouraged to actually dress for their imaginary trips on the day of the activity, i.e., wear western style clothes for western state trips, wear camping clothes for camping trips, etc. Classmates may try guessing each student's destination from the special clothes worn.

Preparation:

Students may create a Fixit Shop by painting a store front on a large piece of cardboard.

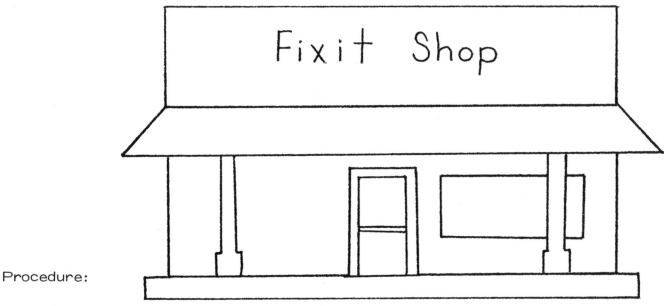

Procedure:

A. Students may select and cut out catalog items which have movable parts.

B. Students may pretend that their selected items are broken. Each may take a turn going to the Fixit Shop and explaining just what is needed to make the item operable. (In essence, the student may tell how the item functions.)

Extension:

Class parents who are repair people may be invited to speak with students about the repair business. A question-answer session may be conducted between students and speakers.

RADIO TALK

Preparation:

    A. Students may cut out a picture of a citizen's band (CB) radio and glue it to a piece of cardboard. The cardboard may be trimmed around the picture. Cardboard supports may be glued to the back of the picture which will allow the picture to be placed in an upright position.

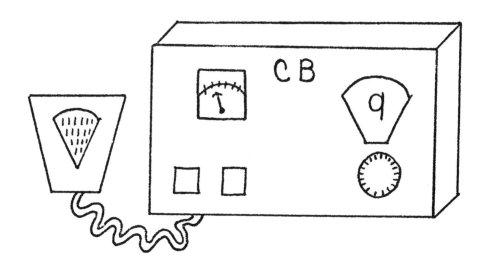

    B. Students may select their own radio call letters and broadcasting names (handles).

Procedure:

    A. Students may organize and name an imaginary radio club.

    B. Students may position themselves around the classroom and pretend to talk with each other through their radios. They may take turns talking about selected topics.

Extension:

Each student may conduct a personal interview of a CB radio owner.

FUNNY TALK

Preparation:

Tape a long piece of mural paper to the wall or chalkboard to be used by students for drawing cartoons.

Procedure:

A. Student pairs may create cartoons with captions on the mural paper by using pictures of catalog models and items.

B. Student pairs may assume the roles of their cartoon characters and read aloud their captions.

Extension:

Students may write a class play to be enacted through cartoon characters drawn on mural paper.

FOR SALE

Preparation:

Transform the classroom into a gigantic garage sale of pictured items. Students may advertise selected items which they have for sale.

Procedure:

A. Direct students to select and cut out one or more pictures of items which they may want to sell at the garage sale. Pictures may be mounted on sheets of writing paper with writing space left below each picture.

B. Direct each student to write an advertisement for selling his or her selected items.

C. Display advertisements around the room where all may be read. Students may decide which is the most convincing and creative ad.

Extension:

A. Students may bring classified sections of newspapers to school and read the "For Sales".

B. Teams of two students may select a catalog item which they want to sell. One student may write a truthful description while the second student may write an exaggerated description. These may be read aloud for comparison.

Preparation:

Assign a different item name to each student. (Items may be selected by simply thumbing through a catalog.) Assigned names may be written on paper and handed to the individual. Item names should not be shared among students.

Procedure:

A. Students may cut out pictures with descriptions of their assigned items.

B. Students may create new names for their assigned items. These names may be substituted for the original name in rewriting each description.

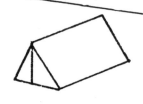

2-person tent. Angled sides. Blue for colorful tent. Zipper front door. Tent has side windows.

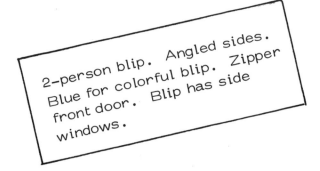

2-person blip. Angled sides. Blue for colorful blip. Zipper front door. Blip has side windows.

C. As students take turns reading their revised descriptions, their classmates may try to identify the original item.

D. The author of the daily riddle may read the proposed solutions (item's identity) written by classmates and show the picture of the item. The student who solved the riddle may become the next day's riddle author.

Extension:

Students may compile booklets of riddles to be exchanged and read by other students.

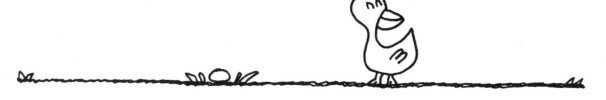

FOOD FOR THOUGHT

Written Expression
Intermediate Level

Preparation:

A. Christmas catalogs or food-item catalogs should be available for this activity. Students may share copies if catalogs are in short supply. (The activity should be more interesting if food pictures are greatly varied.)

B. A food-center space may be created by painting a cabinet front on a large sheet of cardboard. This cardboard may be taped to a wall.

Procedure:

A. Each student may cut out several pictures of food items and paste each to a separate sheet of writing paper.

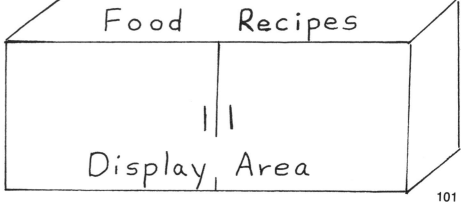

Food   Recipes

Display Area

B. Each student may create and write below the picture a recipe for preparing the food. Recipes may include ingredients and instructions for cooking or baking if needed.

C. Each student may bind pages together in a Recipe Booklet and create a colorful cover for it.

D. Recipe booklets may be displayed on the cardboard cabinet front.

Extension:

A. Students may copy simple recipes from cookbooks and actually prepare foods in class.

B. The activity may be extended to food preservation. Catalog pictures of necessary materials and utensils may be used to illustrate written directions for preserving food.

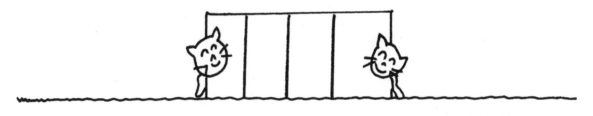

OPENING NIGHT

Written Expression
Intermediate Level

Preparation:

Create a theatre atmosphere by painting a theatre front on a large sheet of cardboard.

Opening Night

(Display Area for Plays)

Procedure:

    A.   Students may select a famous television family and write a play (story episode) for the family. The play may be illustrated with catalog pictures. Encourage students to use various moods in their stories, i.e., happy characters, sad characters, frightened characters, etc.

    B.   Students may display their completed plays on the theatre front.

Extension:

    A.   Plays may be enacted by small groups of students. An "opening night" may be established for each play. Non-acting students may "purchase tickets" for the presentation from a student ticket seller.

    B.   Television episodes may be written and illustrated on mural paper.

    C.   Students may create their own family series for television. Plays may be written for the new series.

SMASHING SLOGANS

| Written Expression |
| Intermediate Level |

Preparation:

    A.   Direct students to read about basics of advertising in reference books.

    B.   Prepare a banner from a length of mural paper for illustrating the name of an imaginary advertising agency.

Procedure:

A. Students may pretend to work for an advertising agency responsible for advertising selected catalog items. Pictures of selected items may be pasted to individual cards.

We Sell Agency

B. Students may write advertising slogans for each of their items.

Keep America Beautiful
Grow with Quick-Gro
Fertilizer

One, two, three
Plant a tree
From Ball's Nursery

C. Students may read completed slogans to classmates and display these slogan cards on the advertising banner.

Extension:

A. Students may use preselected words in writing slogans about given items.

B. Students may write nonsense slogans about famous people.

FUNNY CUT-UPS

Preparation:

    A.   Transform the classroom into a modern art gallery and select a name for the gallery.

    B.   Paint a large building front to simulate an art gallery on cardboard or the chalk board.

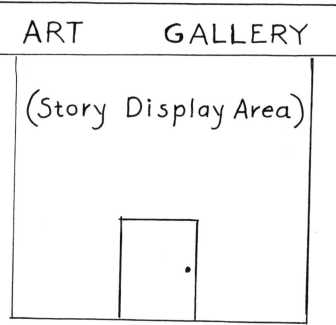

Procedure:

    A.   Students may create an abstract design by cutting up catalog pictures and pasting the pieces on a sheet of writing paper. (Designs may take various forms and shapes, depending on individual abilities and interests.)

    B.   Students may write short stories describing their new creations. (Stories may be written below each art creation.)

    C.   Students may read their stories and hang their art creations on the art gallery front.

Extension:

Names of catalog items may be used as story starters. Students may write stories which have the following starts:

    (1) The funniest bicycle I ever saw was...
    (2) The day the hole fell out of my bowling ball...
    (3) The day the popcorn popper wouldn't stop...

MEET THE PEOPLE

Preparation:

A case history, as defined in this activity, consists of personal data relating to a given individual. Data categories include: name, birth date, birth place, occupation, family, hobbies, previous residential locations, health, etc.

Procedure:

A. Each student may select and cut out one picture of a catalog model. The picture may be pasted to a sheet of writing paper.

B. Each student may then prepare a personal case history of the person pictured.

C. Written case histories may be displayed around the room for other students to read.

Extension:

A. Students may interview community people and write their case histories.

B. Students may write case histories of their classmates.

C. Students may write case histories of famous people based on factual data from reference books.

Preparation:

Students may read about the history and applications of magic from classroom references.

Procedure:

A. Each student may select one catalog item and pretend that it possesses some magical power. A story may be written about the item and its power.

B. A class contest may be conducted for determining which catalog item possesses the greatest power. This may be accomplished by each student reading his or her story while other students decide just how magical the item is.

Extension:

A. Stories about magical items may be exchanged for other students to read.

B. Students may write science fiction stories and illustrate them with catalog pictures.

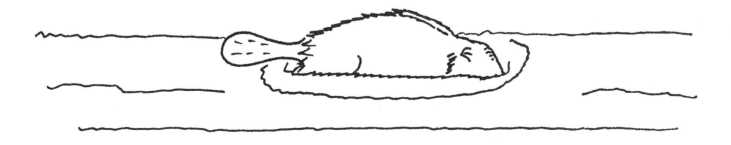

Preparation:

A. Cut out and paste twenty-four pictures of toy items on individual cards. On the back of each, list a dozen words which a student may use in writing a story about the toy.

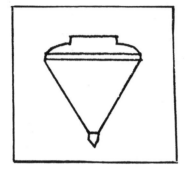

top	fast
wooden	red
spin	twirl
round	floor
pointed	present
fall	blue

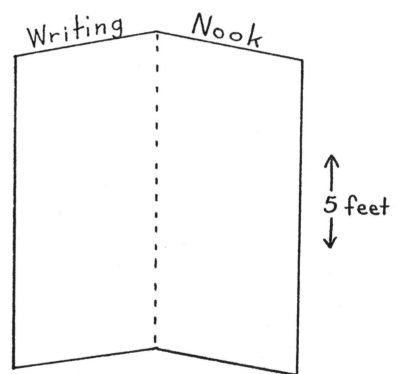

Writing Nook

5 feet

B. Direct students to construct a writing nook by fastening two long sheets of cardboard together along one edge. These may be placed in a vertical position in a corner so that writers may have privacy from the open classroom. A table and chairs may be placed in the nook.

Procedure:

A. Students with free time may go to the writing nook and use one of the picture cards to write a story.

B. Stories may be displayed on the outer walls of the writing nook for other students to read.

Extension:

Students may select a toy card and tell a story about the toy using pre-selected words.

Preparation:

A paper-carton robot may be constructed by students for use in this activity. This robot may provide a place for displaying riddles written by individual students. A small paper box or envelope to be used for depositing possible riddle solutions may be attached to the robot.

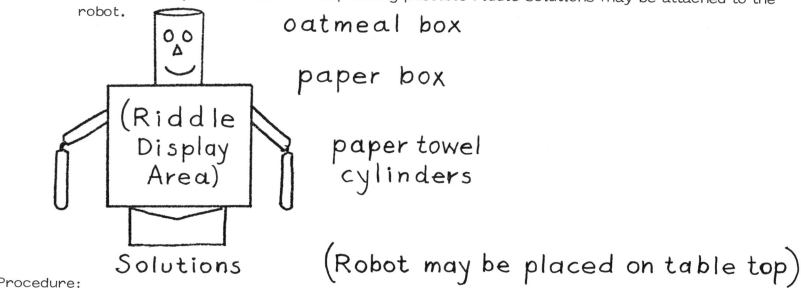

oatmeal box

paper box

paper towel cylinders

Solutions

(Robot may be placed on table top)

Procedure:

A. Students may select items from their catalogs and write a riddle about the identity of each item on a small card.

B. Pictures of riddle items may be cut out by each student and filed for later use.

C. Students may take turns in displaying one riddle card each day on the front of Robot Riddler. Classmates may write possible solutions to the riddle and deposit them in the box or envelope attached to the robot.

"I have four wheels, but no tongue, nor spokes and I'm stood on a lot. What am I?" (answer - skate)

Preparation:

Two blanks for gift cards may be prepared from a standard sheet of construction paper (or duplicating paper) by cutting the sheet along its long edge into equal halves. Each half, when folded, will measure 5-1/2" high and 4-1/4" wide.

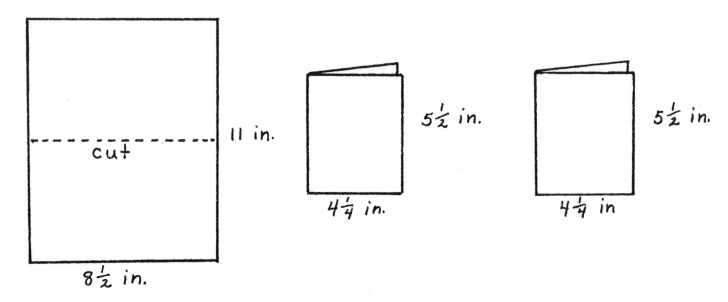

Procedure:

Each student may create gift cards for two special people by writing a personal message on the front of each card and pasting pictures of catalog items on the inside.

Extension:

A.   Gift cards may actually be mailed in envelopes addressed by students.

B. A classroom activity may be started in which students send "I Care" messages
    to other students. These messages may be named Care-O-Grams. A post
    office nook may be created in the classroom for sending and receiving
    Care-O-Grams. Each student may have a box for receiving Care-O-Grams.

PICTURE A STORY

Preparation:

A. Direct students to paste four sheets of writing paper together to form a
    rectangle approximately 16 x 22".

B. Prepare a spirit master with the
    following instructions for writing
    a picture story:

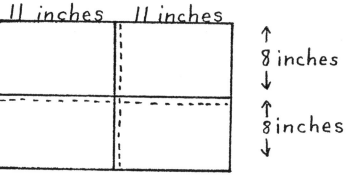

Camping

1. Cut out a blue tent.
2. Place your tent in a forest.
3. Put a mother, father, son, and daughter next to the tent.
4. Place some cooking utensils around a fire close to the tent.
5. Write a story about camping.

Cycling

1. Cut out a bicycle.
2. Place the bicycle on a country road.
3. Put a student next to the bike.
4. Place a spare bicycle wheel on the ground behind the bicycle.
5. Write a story about cycling.

Sports Equipment

1. Cut out pictures of four kinds of sports equipment.
2. Place the equipment on shelves fastened to a wall.
3. Place a boy and a girl next to the shelves.
4. Put a window in the wall on the right side of the shelves.
5. Write a story about sports equipment.

Procedure:

A. Distribute story instructions, assigning the same story to every third student.

B. Students may read story instructions and select appropriate pictures from their catalogs to construct picture stories.

C. Students may present completed stories to the class.

Extension:

Students may write instructions for a picture story to be completed by another student.

112